PicScience Prese
Fractions to Decimals

12.3 14.7 31.5 25.4 8.9

16.2

11.254 44.88 53.3 42.4

5.54 2.4 12.1 21.2

PicScience Presents:

Fractions to Decimals

Including

- ✓ Lesson Material
- ✓ Problem Sets
- ✓ Fractions and Division Review
- ✓ Tips and Tricks for Mastering Fractions
- ✓ Solutions

And More!

FREE fractions help including practice worksheets and solutions.

www.picscience.net/free-resources

Have you completed <u>Fractions for Beginners</u>? We recommend it for students that are just starting to learn about fractions. Check it out and more on our website above.

Contents

Let's Review Fractions

A fraction is part of a whole or part of a group.

Part of a whole

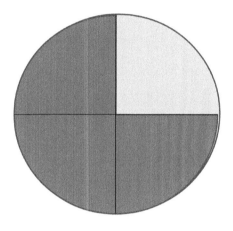

$\dfrac{3}{4}$ of the circle is blue

Part of a group

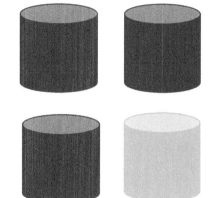

$\dfrac{3}{4}$ of the group is purple

Let's Review Fractions

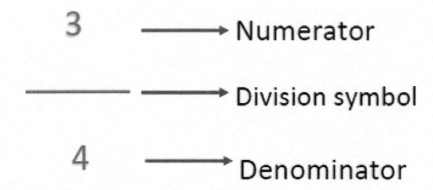

- The top number is the **numerator**

- The bottom number is the **denominator**

- The line that separates the numerator (3) from the denominator (4) is a **division symbol**. It tells us that we can divide these two numbers.

Let's Review Fractions

Let's review some division before we go on. We'll have to understand division well to divide the numerator by the denominator in a fraction. All the expressions below are the same.

Written	Expression 1	Expression 2	Expression 3	Expression 4
12 divided by 3 is 4	$\dfrac{12}{3} = 4$	$12/3 = 4$	$3\overline{)12} = 4$	$12 \div 3 = 4$
10 divided by 2 is 5	$\dfrac{10}{2} = 5$	$10/2 = 5$	$2\overline{)10} = 5$	$10 \div 2 = 5$
20 divided by 4 is 5	$\dfrac{20}{4} = 5$	$20/4 = 5$	$4\overline{)20} = 5$	$20 \div 4 = 5$
6 divided by 2 is 3	$\dfrac{6}{2} = 3$	$6/2 = 3$	$2\overline{)6} = 3$	$6 \div 2 = 3$
4 divided by 1 is 4	$\dfrac{4}{1} = 4$	$4/1 = 4$	$1\overline{)4} = 4$	$4 \div 1 = 4$

Do-Now Exercise

Find the simplest form of the fractions below.

1. $2\overline{)8}=$

2. $3\overline{)6}=$

3. $3\overline{)15}=$

4. $7\overline{)14}=$

5. $4\overline{)12}=$

6. $5\overline{)10}=$

7. $2\overline{)12}=$

8. $3\overline{)12}=$

9. $5\overline{)20}=$

10. $4\overline{)24}=$

Solutions

1. 4

2. 2

3. 5

4. 2

5. 3

6. 2

7. 6

8. 4

9. 4

10. 6

Chapter 1

Reading and Writing Fractions as Decimals

Fractions and Decimals

- A **decimal** is another way of representing a fraction.

- A decimal has no numerator or denominator.

- The period (.) represents the decimal point.

- We can read five-tenths as 0.5.

- For example, the fraction $\frac{5}{10}$ can be expressed as a decimal, **0.5**.

Writing Fractions as Decimals

- Fractions with 10, 100, or 1000 in the denominator can be represented as decimals.

$$\frac{1}{10} = 0.1 \qquad \frac{1}{100} = 0.01 \qquad \frac{1}{1000} = 0.001$$

- The fraction $\frac{1}{10}$ can be expressed as 0.1 or one-tenth.

- The fraction $\frac{1}{100}$ can be expressed as 0.01 or one-hundredth.

- The fraction $\frac{1}{1000}$ can be expressed as 0.001 or one-thousandth.

Reading and Writing Fractions as Decimals

	Tens	Hundreds	Thousands
Fraction	$\dfrac{1}{10}$	$\dfrac{1}{100}$	$\dfrac{1}{1000}$
Decimal	0.1	0.01	0.001

Writing Fractions as Decimals

- For fractions with a denominator of 10, the decimal is expressed as tenths.

$$\frac{1}{10} = 0.1$$

- For 1/10 we write the decimal point (.) and then the numerator. In this example, the numerator is 1. It takes the tenths position, so the decimal is written as one-tenth and read as 0.1.

- The places after the decimal point are called **decimal places**.

Reading and Writing Fractions
as Decimals

Fraction	Decimal	Decimal places	Written
$\dfrac{9}{10}$	0.9	1 decimal place	Nine-tenths
$\dfrac{23}{100}$	0.23	2 decimal places	Twenty-three-hundreds
$\dfrac{765}{1000}$	0.765	3 decimal places	Seven hundred-sixty-five-thousandths

Take a look at the chart above:

* The decimal 0.9 has 1 decimal place.

* The decimal 0.23 has 2 decimal places.

* The decimal 0.765 has 3 decimal places.

Writing Fractions as Decimals

Example 1: Write the fraction $\frac{1}{10}$ as a decimal.

Let's find the decimal that is equal to $\frac{1}{10}$. We can start with the denominator.

- The denominator is 10. So, we know that the new decimal will be in the tenths place.

- The numerator is 1, so we can place the 1 in the tenths place.

$$\frac{1}{10} = 0.1$$

Tenths

Writing Fractions as Decimals

Example 2: Write the fraction $\frac{7}{10}$ as a decimal.

Let's find the decimal that is equal to $\frac{7}{10}$. We can start with the denominator.

- The denominator is 10. So, we know that the new decimal will be in the tenths place.

- The numerator is 7, so we can place the 7 in the tenths place.

$$\frac{7}{10} = 0.7$$

$\downarrow$

Tenths

Writing Fractions as Decimals

Example 3: Write the fraction $\frac{23}{100}$ as a decimal.

Let's find the decimal that is equal to $\frac{23}{100}$. We can start with the denominator.

- The denominator is 100. So, we know that the new decimal will have two decimal places because it is in the hundredths place.

- The numerator is 21, so we can place the 2 in the tenths place and the 1 in the hundredths place. Therefore, the new decimal is 0.21.

Note: If a fraction has 100 in the denominator, the equivalent decimal will have two decimal places.

$$\frac{23}{100} = 0.\ 2\ \ 3$$

Tenths

Hundreths

Writing Fractions as Decimals

Example 3: Write the fraction $\frac{153}{1000}$ as a decimal.

Let's find the decimal that is equal to $\frac{153}{1000}$. We can start with the denominator.

- The denominator is 1000. So, we know that the new decimal will have three decimal places because it is in the thousandths place.

- The numerator is 153, so we can place 1 in the tenths place, 5 in the hundredths place, and 3 in the thousandths place. Therefore, the new decimal is 0.153.

Note: If a fraction has 1000 in the denominator, the equivalent decimal will have three decimal places.

$$\frac{153}{1000} = 0.\ 1\ \ 5\ \ 3$$

Tenths   Thousandths

Hundreths

Do-Now Exercises

Write the following fractions as decimals.

1. $\dfrac{1}{100} =$

2. $\dfrac{3}{10} =$

3. $\dfrac{5}{10} =$

4. $\dfrac{4}{100} =$

5. $\dfrac{50}{100} =$

6. $\dfrac{35}{100} =$

7. $\dfrac{7}{10} =$

8. $\dfrac{9}{10} =$

9. $\dfrac{23}{100} =$

10. $\dfrac{90}{100} =$

Solutions

Write the following fractions as decimals.

1. 0.01

2. 0.3

3. 0.5

4. 0.04

5. 0.50

6. 0.35

7. 0.7

8. 0.9

9. 0.23

10. 0.90

Chapter 2

Converting Fractions to Decimals

$$\frac{3}{4} \quad = \quad 0.75$$

Converting Fractions to Decimals with Division

When the fraction has 10, 100, or 1000 in the denominator, we can rewrite that fraction as a decimal, as we've done in the previous sections.

But with other fractions, we may need to use division to convert them to decimals.

- A fraction is made up of two parts: a numerator and a denominator. It is used to represent the number of parts selected out of the total number of parts.

- As we saw earlier, the line in a fraction that separates the numerator and denominator can be rewritten using the division symbol.

- So, to convert a fraction to a decimal, divide the numerator by the denominator. This will give us our answer as a decimal.

Converting Fractions to Decimals with Division

It is important to master expressing fractions in different ways.

- When given a fraction, place the numerator inside the division symbol. This is called the dividend.

- When given a fraction, place the denominator on the outside of the division symbol. This is called the divisor.

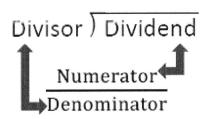

Note: Look at the table on page 7 to see more examples of expressing fractions in different ways.

Converting Fractions to Decimals with Division

Example 1: Convert the fraction $\frac{2}{5}$ to a decimal.

<u>Goal</u>: Long division to get to no remainders.

$$\frac{2}{5} = 5\overline{)2}$$

Step 1: We know that 5 does not go into 2 at all.

However, 5 does go into 20. We know this because you can multiply 5 x 4 = 20 (this means that 5 goes into 20, <u>4 times</u>).

Step 2: Next, you subtract 20 from 20 like this 20 − 20 = 0. Now you have no remainders left over.

Converting Fractions to Decimals with Division

Example 1: Convert the fraction $\frac{2}{5}$ to a decimal. Let's look at how the steps on the previous page are carried out.

Step 1:

$$
\begin{array}{r}
0.4 \uparrow \\
5 \,)\overline{2.0}
\end{array}
$$

Step 2:

$$
\begin{array}{r}
-20 \\
\hline
0
\end{array}
$$

So, the fraction $\frac{2}{5}$ is **0.4** as a decimal.

Converting Fractions to Decimals with Division

Look at the chart below. The fractions on the left are represented as decimals on the right. Both are equivalent.

Fraction	Decimal
$\dfrac{4}{5}$	0.8
$\dfrac{75}{100}$	0.75
$\dfrac{3}{6}$	0.5

Let's practice basic division and then look closer at more examples of converting fractions to decimals on the following pages.

Do-Now Exercise

Solve the division problems.

1. $16 \div 4 =$

2. $14 \div 2 =$

3. $8 \div 2 =$

4. $12 \div 2 =$

5. $15 \div 3 =$

6. $21 \div 7 =$

7. $18 \div 9 =$

8. $24 \div 3 =$

9. $48 \div 2 =$

10. $9 \div 3 =$

Solutions

Write the following fractions as decimals.

1. 4

2. 7

3. 4

4. 6

5. 5

6. 3

7. 2

8. 8

9. 24

10. 3

Chapter 3

Using Long Division to Convert Fractions to Decimals

$$\frac{4}{5} = 5\overline{)4.00} = 0.8$$

Converting Fractions to Decimals with Long Division

Example 1: Convert the fraction $\frac{4}{5}$ to a decimal.

Written	Expression 1	Expression 2	Expression 3
4 divided by 5	$\frac{4}{5}$	$4/5$	$5\overline{)4}$

Let's take a closer look at converting the fraction 4/5 into a decimal. We can use long division with Expression 3 in the table.

Converting Fractions to Decimals with Long Division (Tenths)

Example 1: Convert the fraction $\frac{4}{5}$ to a decimal.

<u>Goal</u>: Long division to get to no remainders.

$$\frac{4}{5} = 5\overline{)4}$$

Step 1: We know that 5 does not go into 4 at all.

However, 5 does go into 40. We know this because you can multiply 5 x 8 = 40 (this means that 5 goes into 40, <u>8 times</u>).

Step 2: Next, you subtract 40 from 40 like this 40 − 40 = 0. Now you have no remainders left over.

Converting Fractions to Decimals with Long Division (Tenths)

Example 1: Convert the fraction $\frac{4}{5}$ to a decimal. Let's look at how the steps on the previous page are carried out.

$$
\begin{array}{r}
0.8 \\
\uparrow \\
\hline
5\overline{)4.0} \\
-40 \\
\hline
0
\end{array}
$$

Step 1:

Step 2:

So, the fraction $\frac{4}{5}$ is 0.8 as a decimal.

Converting Fractions to Decimals with Long Division (Tenths)

Example 1: Convert the fraction $\frac{2}{5}$ to a decimal.

<u>Goal</u>: Long division to get to no remainders.

$$\frac{2}{5} = 5\overline{)2}$$

Step 1: We know that 5 does not go into 2 at all.

However, 5 does go into 20. We know this because you can multiply 5 x 4 = 20 (this means that 5 goes into 20, <u>4 times</u>).

Step 2: Next, you subtract 20 from 20 like this 20 − 20 = 0. Now you have no remainders left over.

Converting Fractions to Decimals with Long Division (Tenths)

Example 1: Convert the fraction $\frac{2}{5}$ to a decimal. Let's look at how the steps on the previous page are carried out.

$$\begin{array}{r} 0.4 \\ 5{\overline{\smash{)}2.0}} \end{array}$$

Step 1:

Step 2:
$$\begin{array}{r} -20 \\ \hline 0 \end{array}$$

So, the fraction $\frac{2}{5}$ is 0.4 as a decimal.

Converting Fractions to Decimals with Long Division (Hundredths)

Example 1: Convert the fraction $\frac{3}{4}$ to a decimal.

<u>Goal</u>: Long division to get to no remainders.

$$\frac{3}{4} = 4\overline{)3}$$

Step 1: We know that 4 does not go into 3 at all. However, 4 does go into 30. We know this because you can multiply 4 x 7 = 28 (this means that 4 goes into 30, <u>7 times</u>).

Step 2: Next, you subtract 28 from 30 like this 30 - 28 = 2. Now, you bring down the 0. Remember our goal is to get to the point that we have no remainders.

Step 3: So to get no remainders we need to complete the last step. This time, 4 goes into 20 exactly 5 times and we will have nothing left over.

Converting Fractions to Decimals with Long Division (Hundredths)

Example 1: Convert the fraction $\frac{3}{4}$ to a decimal. Let's look at how the steps on the previous page are carried out.

$$
\begin{array}{r}
0.75 \\
\uparrow \\
4\,\overline{)\,3.00} \\
-2\,8 \\
\hline
20 \\
-20 \\
\hline
0
\end{array}
$$

Step 1:

Step 2:

Step 3:

So, the fraction $\frac{3}{4}$ is 0.75 as a decimal.

Converting Fractions to Decimals with Long Division (Hundredths)

Example 1: Convert the fraction $\frac{1}{4}$ to a decimal.

<u>Goal</u>: Long division to get to no remainders.

$$\frac{1}{4} = 4\overline{)1}$$

Step 1: We know that 4 does not go into 1 at all. However, 4 does go into 10. We know this because you can multiply 4 x 2 = 8 (this means that 4 goes into 10, <u>2 times</u>).

Step 2: Next, you subtract 8 from 10 like this 10 - 8 = 2. Now, you bring down the 0. Remember our goal is to get to the point that we have no remainders.

Step 3: So to get no remainders we need to complete the last step. This time, 4 goes into 20 exactly 5 times and we will have nothing left over.

Converting Fractions to Decimals with Long Division (Hundredths)

Example 1: Convert the fraction $\frac{1}{4}$ to a decimal. Let's look at how the steps on the previous page are carried out.

$$
\begin{array}{r}
0.25 \\
4\overline{)1.00} \\
\end{array}
$$

Step 1:

$$4\,\overline{)1.00}$$

Step 2:

$$-8$$

$$20$$

Step 3:

$$-20$$

$$0$$

So, the fraction $\frac{1}{4}$ is 0.25 as a decimal.

Do-Now Exercise

Convert the following fractions to decimals.

1. $\dfrac{3}{5} =$

2. $\dfrac{4}{5} =$

3. $\dfrac{2}{4} =$

4. $\dfrac{3}{6} =$

5. $\dfrac{1}{5} =$

6. $\dfrac{4}{5} =$

7. $\dfrac{3}{4} =$

8. $\dfrac{9}{20} =$

9. $\dfrac{6}{25} =$

10. $\dfrac{7}{50} =$

Solutions

Write the following fractions as decimals.

1. 0.6

2. 0.8

3. 0.5

4. 0.5

5. 0.2

6. 0.8

7. 0.75

8. 0.45

9. 0.24

10. 0.14

Chapter 4

Converting Decimals to Fractions

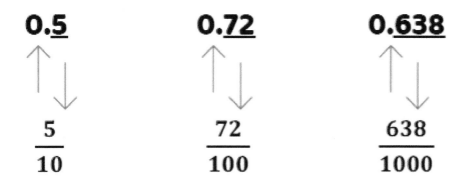

Writing Decimals as Fractions

Example 1: Write the decimal 0.08 as a fraction.

Step 1:

Let's find the numerator of the new fraction.

- The number after the decimal point is 8, so we place 8 in the numerator.

Step 2:

Let's find the denominator of the new fraction.

- We start by writing 1 in the denominator when converting this decimal to a fraction.

- Find the number of decimal places after the decimal point. For example, in 0.08, there are two decimal places. So, we add two zeros next to the 1. The denominator is 100.

Writing Decimals as Fractions

Example 1: Write the decimal 0.08 as a fraction.

Step 3:

With 8 in the numerator and 100 in the denominator, the new fraction is $\frac{8}{100}$.

$$0.08 = \frac{8}{100}$$

Simplifying Fractions

You may be asked to write the decimal as a fraction in its simplest form.

Example 2: Write the decimal 0.30 as a fraction in its simplest form.

Step 1:

Let's find the numerator of the new fraction.

- The number after the decimal point is 30, so we place 30 in the numerator.

Step 2:

Let's find the denominator of the new fraction.

- We start by writing 1 in the denominator when converting this decimal to a fraction.

- Find the number of decimal places after the decimal point. For example, in 0.30, there are two decimal places. So, we add two zeros next to the 1. The denominator is 100.

Step 3:

- With 3 in the numerator and 100 in the denominator, the new fraction is 30/100.

- Now, we are ready to simplify this fraction.

Step 4:

- Find the **Greatest Common Factor (GCF)** of 30 and 100. The GCF is a factor you can divide both numbers by.
    - Factors of 30: 1, 2, 5, 6, ⑩ 15, 30
    - Factors of 100: 1, 2, 4, 5, ⑩ 25, 50, 100

Step 5:

- Divide the numerator and denominator by the GCF of 10 to solve for the simplest form.

$$\frac{30}{100} \div \frac{10}{10} = \frac{3}{10}$$

$$0.30 = \frac{30}{100} = \frac{3}{10}$$

Writing Decimals as Fractions

Example 3: Write the decimal 0.4 as a fraction.

Step 1:

Let's find the numerator of the new fraction.

- The number after the decimal point is 4, so we place 4 in the numerator.

Step 2:

Let's find the denominator of the new fraction.

- We start by writing 1 in the denominator when converting this decimal to a fraction.

- Find the number of decimal places after the decimal point. For example, in 0.08, there is only one decimal place. So, we place one zero next to the 1. The denominator is 10.

Writing Decimals as Fractions

Example 3: Write the decimal 0.4 as a fraction.

Step 3:

With 4 in the numerator and 10 in the denominator, the new fraction is $\frac{4}{10}$.

$$0.4 = \frac{4}{10}$$

Writing Decimals as Fractions

Example 4: Write the decimal 0.35 as a fraction.

Step 1:

Let's find the numerator of the new fraction.

- The number after the decimal point is 35, so we place 35 in the numerator.

Step 2:

Let's find the denominator of the new fraction.

- We start by writing 1 in the denominator when converting this decimal to a fraction.

- Find the number of decimal places after the decimal point. For example, in 0.35, there are two decimal places. So, we place two zeroes next to the 1. The denominator is 100.

Writing Decimals as Fractions

Example 4: Write the decimal 0.35 as a fraction.

Step 3:

With 35 in the numerator and 100 in the denominator, the new fraction is $\frac{35}{100}$.

$$0.35 = \frac{35}{100}$$

Writing Decimals as Fractions

Example 5: Write the decimal 0.002 as a fraction.

Step 1:

Let's find the numerator of the new fraction.

- The number after the decimal point is 2, so we place 2 in the numerator.

Step 2:

Let's find the denominator of the new fraction.

- We start by writing 1 in the denominator when converting this decimal to a fraction.

- Find the number of decimal places after the decimal point. For example, in 0.002, there are three decimal places. So, we place three zeroes next to the 1. The denominator is 1000.

Writing Decimals as Fractions

Example 5: Write the decimal 0.002 as a fraction.

Step 3:

With 2 in the numerator and 1000 in the denominator, the new fraction is $\frac{2}{1000}$.

$$0.002 = \frac{2}{1000}$$

Converting Decimals to Fractions

We know that we can convert decimals to fractions and vice versa. So, let's take a closer look at this example below and convert the decimal to the fraction.

Example 1: 0.3 (three-tenths) = $\frac{3}{10}$

Step 1:

Write down 0.3 divided by 1 like this $\frac{0.3}{1}$

Note: Placing a decimal over 1 does not change the value.

Step 2:

Multiply both the numerator and the denominator by a whole number. Use 10 (because there is 1 digit after the decimal place)

$$\frac{0.3}{1} \times \frac{10}{10} = \frac{3}{10}$$

Note: Do you see how it changes the numerator to a whole number?

The decimal 0.3 is the fraction $\frac{3}{10}$

Converting Decimals to Fractions

Example 2: 0.9 (nine-tenths) = $\frac{9}{10}$

Step 1:

Write down 0.9 divided by 1 like this $\frac{0.9}{1}$

Note: *Placing a decimal over 1 does not change the value.*

Step 2:

Multiply both the numerator and the denominator by a whole number. Use 10 (because there is 1 digit after the decimal place)

$$\frac{0.9}{1} \times \frac{10}{10} = \frac{9}{10}$$

Note: *Do you see how it changes the numerator to a whole number?*

The decimal 0.9 is the fraction $\frac{9}{10}$

Converting Decimals to Fractions

Example 3: 0.04 (four-hundredths) = $\frac{4}{100}$

Step 1:

Write down 0.04 divided by 1 like this $\frac{0.04}{1}$

Note: Placing a decimal over 1 does not change the value.

Step 2:

Multiply both the numerator and the denominator by a whole number. Use 100 (because there are 2 digits after the decimal place)

$$\frac{0.04}{1} \times \frac{100}{100} = \frac{4}{100}$$

Note: Do you see how it changes the numerator to a whole number?

The decimal 0.04 is the fraction $\frac{4}{100}$

Do-Now Exercise

Convert the following decimals to fractions.

1. 0.2

2. 0.41

3. 0.03

4. 0.7

5. 0.09

6. 0.3

7. 0.6

8. 0.23

9. 0.5

10. 0.8

Solutions

Convert the following decimals to fractions.

1. $\dfrac{2}{10}$

2. $\dfrac{41}{100}$

3. $\dfrac{3}{100}$

4. $\dfrac{7}{10}$

5. $\dfrac{9}{100}$

6. $\dfrac{3}{10}$

7. $\dfrac{6}{10}$

8. $\dfrac{23}{100}$

9. $\dfrac{5}{10}$

10. $\dfrac{8}{10}$

Concept Review

The next few pages will test how well you understand the concepts in this book.

Try the Problem Below

1. Write a decimal and a fraction for the shaded parts.

Hint: How many total parts are there?

Try the Problem Below

2. Which of the following is equivalent to $\frac{2}{5}$?

    A.   0.1

    B.   0.2

    C.   0.4

    D.   0.6

Hint: Find an equivalent fraction with 10 in the denominator.

Try the Problem Below

3. Express the following statement as a fraction and as a decimal. A total of 6 out of 100 players on the chess team did not finish the game.

Hint: Read a decimal by reading the place value of the last digit at the right.

Try the Problem Below

4. Which of the following is equivalent to 0.83?

   A. $8\dfrac{3}{10}$

   B. $8\dfrac{3}{100}$

   C. $\dfrac{83}{100}$

   D. $\dfrac{83}{10}$

Try the Problem Below

5. Which decimal is equivalent to $\frac{1}{4}$?

    A.   0.14

    B.   0.25

    C.   0.20

    D.   0.75

Hint: Find an equivalent fraction with 100 in the denominator.

Try the Problem Below

6. This year, 100 people are playing the game. Of this number, 30 people have never played before. How can you express this part of the group as a fraction and as a decimal?

Solutions

1. There are 10 total parts in the shape

    Fraction: $\frac{6}{10}$

    Decimal: 0.6

2. **0.4**

    To find an equivalent fraction with 10 in the denominator:

    Multiply $\frac{2}{5}$ by $\frac{2}{2}$

    $$\frac{2}{5} \times \frac{2}{2} = \frac{4}{10}$$

3. The answer is six-hundredths.

    Fraction: $\frac{6}{100}$

    Decimal: 0.06

4. $\dfrac{83}{100}$

- The first number after the decimal point is 83. So, the numerator is 83.

- The last digit, 3, is in the hundredths place. So, the denominator is 100.

5. 0.25

- Because the answer has a decimal in hundredths, let's find an equivalent fraction with 100 in the denominator.

$$\frac{1}{4} = \frac{1 \times 25}{4 \times 25} = \frac{25}{100} = 0.25 \times 0.01 = 0.25$$

6. The answer is thirty-hundredths.

Fraction: $\dfrac{30}{100}$

Decimal: 0.30

Certificate of Completion

THIS IS TO CERTIFY THAT

has successfully completed PicScience's Fractions
to Decimals workbook

Page Jones

Page Jones, PhD

PROGRAM INSTRUCTOR

Hanna Jones

Hanna Jones

PROGRAM INSTRUCTOR

Printed in Great Britain
by Amazon

78174180R20045